TO FEEL
anything
AT ALL

*your thoughts deserve
a decent place
to live*

also by R. Clift

evolved poetry series
TO BE REMEMBERED

UNTIL WE MEET AGAIN
YOUR THOUGHTS DESERVE A DECENT PLACE TO LIVE

TO

FEEL

ANYTHING

AT

ALL

For Art

WITHOUT YOU, MY WORDS WOULD HAVE
NEVER FOUND THEIR COURAGE
TO BE HEARD.

WHAT IS AN EVOLVED POEM?

Photography is how I see the world,
poetry is how I interpret it.
I wished to meld my two passions together–
so this project was born.

For this summer series, I chose a handful of poems,
two dear friends, and took them to secluded locations in
nature to explore and shoot.
In short, we read the poems one by one, pinpointed the
feeling from the words and found a way
to recreate that feeling visually in a photograph.

These photos are essentially, themselves, poems.

I'd like to thank the exquisite Olivia and Vanessa for
following me deep into the woods, across rivers, and
over the tops of mountains all for the sake of art, poetry,
and human emotion.

xx –R

r.clift

*The sky has a way of
taking care of me —*

WHEN I'M LONELY
THE SUNLIGHT CARESSES MY SKIN

WHEN I HAVE NO ONE ELSE TO TALK TO
THE MOON IS THERE TO LISTEN

WHEN I'M SAD THE RAIN FALLS
SO I DON'T HAVE TO CRY ALONE

AND WHEN I'M LOST, OR AFRAID
THE STARS GUIDE ME HOME

TO FEEL anything AT ALL

IT IS BOTH SAD AND COMFORTING TO KNOW
YOUR VOICE WILL CARRY FARTHER
THAN YOUR FEET WILL EVER TAKE YOU,

YOUR WORDS WILL LIVE ON IN THE
MEMORIES OF OTHERS AND THE PAGES YOU'VE
FILLED LONG AFTER WE'VE GONE—

ALTHOUGH IT'S TRUE, WE CANNOT
LIVE FOREVER
(we can't even live for long)

YOUR PRINTED THOUGHTS, YOUR
UNDERSTANDING OF THIS WORLD,
THE INK THAT BLEEDS FROM YOUR VEINS

IS ETERNAL

r.clift

if the stars can wait
 for you to find
 your way back —

so can i

TO FEEL *anything* AT ALL

WHEN I CLOSE MY EYES I FIND MYSELF
ON COBBLESTONE STREETS, SOMEWHERE
BETWEEN THE DIRT AND THE STARS
AND ALL THAT THE UNIVERSE IS MADE OF
DREAMING OF SOMETHING MORE
SOMETHING I CANNOT HAVE
SOMETHING I HAVE RESIGNED MYSELF
TO GIVING UP
BECAUSE SOMEWHERE ALONG THE WAY
SOMEONE TOLD ME I WASN'T
GOOD ENOUGH AND I WAS THE
FOOL THAT BELIEVED THEM

SO NOW MY EYES ARE OPEN AND
I LOOK INTO THE MIRROR AND I WANT
MORE THAN ANYTHING TO BE HAPPY WITH
WHO I AM BUT THERE IS NOTHING
MORE THAT I WANT THAN TO BE
SOMETHING MORE
something magnificent

AND AS THE STARS REFLECT IN
MY EYES I WONDER IF MAYBE
I ALREADY AM

r.clift

the heart of any thing

EVERYTHING CAN BE ANYTHING
AND ANYTHING CAN BE NOTHING
BUT EVERYTHING CANNOT BE NOTHING
OR NOTHING WOULD BE ANYTHING

SO WHAT IS IT WHEN SOMETHING
IS YOUR EVERYTHING, BUT TO HIM
THAT SOMETHING IS NOTHING, BECAUSE
THAT SOMETHING IS THE SAME AS
ANYTHING HE HAS HELD BEFORE AND
SO YOUR EVERYTHING
FEELS LIKE NOTHING.

SO WHAT THING THEN MEANS ANYTHING
IF IT DOESN'T MEAN EVERYTHING
TO EVERYONE.
LISTEN CLOSELY—
IT DOESN'T MATTER IF YOUR SOMETHING
MEANS NOTHING TO HIM, TO THEM,
IF IT MEANS EVERYTHING TO YOU

THEN IT IS
YOU ARE
SO VERY ENOUGH

and the best thing i can give to you now
is the truth that
if you look to others for happiness,

you will always be disappointed.

INSTEAD
LOOK
WITHIN

LIKE THE SUN
YOU WILL ALWAYS
be rising

TO FEEL *anything* AT ALL

DO YOU EVER MISS FALLING IN LOVE?

THE SHORT BREATHS, THE FLUTTERS
IN YOUR STOMACH, THE TINY
HEARTACHES WHEN YOU SAY GOODNIGHT,

*and the idea that being alive
is about more than just being alive*

r.clift

she isn't like the others —

she revisits her favorite books
like old friends

and relies on tea
to keep her warm.

TO FEEL *anything* AT ALL

HER HEART
IS LIKE A CAGED BIRD
ENCASED IN HER RIBS
UNABLE TO BREAK FREE

IT BEATS
AGAINST THE BARS
AND LONGS TO SPREAD
ITS WINGS

it's dying of loneliness
BUT IT STILL SINGS

TO FEEL *anything* AT ALL

EVERY ONCE IN A WHILE
YOU'LL WALK INTO MY DREAM
AND DIG UP THAT PART OF MY HEART
I TRIED SO VERY HARD TO HIDE,

AND IT'S HIGHLY UNFAIR
because i wake up in love with you
AND YOU'LL NEVER BE THERE.

I THOUGHT THE HARDEST THING I WOULD EVER DO WAS WALK AWAY FROM YOU, BUT IN TRUTH— WHAT HURT THE MOST, WAS WATCHING YOU FALL IN LOVE WITH SOMEONE ELSE

r.clift

I CAN STILL FEEL HIS HANDS
ON MY SKIN
ALTHOUGH
his voice
I CAN'T REMEMBER

HIS BODY
NEXT TO MINE
HAUNTS MY MEMORY
BUT
I CAN'T RECALL
HIS LAUGHTER

I'D GIVE UP EVERY KISS
IN AN INSTANT
TO REMEMBER
THE WAY HE
SAID MY NAME

TO FEEL *anything* AT ALL

DURING THE DAY IT'S EASY TO FORGET,
IT'S EASY TO GO ABOUT MY LIFE
AND PRETEND I WASN'T FALLING FOR YOU—
AFTER THE SUN SETS, HOWEVER,
i crumble
WHEN THE ONLY THING
I CAN PULL AROUND ME IS
A THIN SHEET
AND WHEN I TURN OVER AND OPEN MY EYES
TO LOOK FOR WHERE YOU SHOULD BE
THE ROOM IS EMPTY
I'M CHILLING FROM THE INSIDE OUT
AND THIS PILE OF BLANKETS
CANNOT KEEP ME WARM

r.clift

MY LOVE FOUND ITS WAY INTO YOUR HEART—
IT STARTED UNPACKING, READY TO MOVE IN
AND LIVE THERE
BUT WHEN YOU GOT HOME YOU
PANICKED, THREW IT OUT AND
LOCKED THE DOOR

YOU FEARED TOO MUCH THE POSSIBILITY
OF LOSING SOMETHING YOU DIDN'T REALIZE
was already yours.

JUST BECAUSE YOU'RE NOT USED TO HAVING
SOMEONE ELSE'S LOVE SETTLE DOWN
IN YOUR HEART— THAT DOESN'T MEAN
THAT'S NOT WHERE IT BELONGS.

YOU PULL ME TOWARDS YOU
LIKE AN INESCAPABLE RIPTIDE,
KISSING ME AS THE WAVES
KISS THE SHORE—
steadily

IN YOUR EYES I LOSE MYSELF
IN THE OCEAN DEEP
AND AS I DROWN
IN YOUR WARMTH

I DON'T EVEN THINK ABOUT
COMING UP FOR AIR

r.clift

PLEASE BE CAREFUL WHEN YOU
FIND YOUR ARMS AROUND ME
for i so easily
FALL IN LOVE

DO NOT TREAT ME LIKE
I AM FRAGILE
I'M MADE OF STRONGER THINGS
THAN GLASS
SO HOLD ME—
tighter
UNTIL YOU LAY FINGERPRINTS
ON MY BONES

TO FEEL *anything* AT ALL

I'VE NEVER MET SOMEONE SO SIMILAR
TO THE OCEAN—
STRONG LIKE THE WAVES YET
GENTLE AS SEA MIST

DEEP, DARK AS THE CAVERNS
YET PLAYFUL AS TIDEPOOLS

*did the water teach you how
to surround people in love?*

DID YOU LEARN PERSISTENCE FROM
WATCHING THE TIDE COME BACK
NO MATTER HOW MANY TIMES IT WAS
SENT AWAY?

I WONDER IF YOU REALIZE HOW MUCH
WE NEED YOU, OR IF LIKE THE OCEAN
YOUR PURPOSE ON THIS EARTH
ISN'T TO JUST BE NEEDED BY PEOPLE—

BUT TO JUST BE, AND BE MAGNIFICENT,
WHETHER WE ARE WATCHING OR NOT.

r.clift

SHE WOULD RATHER BE LOST— WANDERING FREELY IN THAT PLACE BETWEEN SLEEP AND AWAKE, WHERE REALITY IS STILL HAZY LIKE A MISTY MORNING SKY, AND EVERYONE IS STILL TOO TIRED TO LIE

TO FEEL *anything* AT ALL

YOU'RE STANDING ON THIS SHORE OF FAMILIARITY
WITH THE INESCAPABLE NEED TO VENTURE
INTO NEW WATERS,
BUT THAT MEANS SAYING GOODBYE
TO THE PLACES YOU'VE KNOWN, THE PEOPLE
WHO MAKE YOU FEEL COMFORTABLE, AND
TO THIS VERY VERSION OF YOURSELF.

YOUR HANDS TREMBLE
AS YOU STARE DOWN AT THE CHOPPY
SEAS BUT EVEN WITH KNOTS IN YOUR
CHEST YOU FIND THE WATER ENTICING
BECAUSE FOR SO LONG
you've been dying for a swim.

THE WATER WILL BE COLD AND THE JOURNEY
WILL BE DIFFICULT BUT WHEN YOU
COME OUT ON THE OTHER SIDE
YOU WILL BE BETTER FOR IT.
SO, MY LOVE, DIVE.

r.clift

I DON'T REMEMBER MUCH BEFORE THE JUMP
I SUPPOSE I RAN
MAYBE I SPRINTED
I DO RECALL BEING SUSPENDED IN THE AIR—
IT WAS MERELY A MOMENT OF FALLING
BUT IT FELT LIKE A LIFETIME OF FLYING
I EXPECTED THE WATER TO BE COLD
IT WASN'T
I EXPECTED THE SALT TO HURT MY EYES
IT DIDN'T
EFFERVESCENCE CLOUDED THE SEA
IT CLEARED AND THE WATER WAS AS BLUE
AS A DREAM.
THE WAVES WERE STRONGER THAN THEY
SEEMED FROM ABOVE
MY HEAD BOBBED ABOVE THE SURFACE AND I
GASPED FOR AIR. THE AIR WAS GOLDEN—
WARM AND SWEET
i realized i had been holding my breath
SINCE LONG BEFORE MY FEET LEFT THE GROUND

I TOOK MY FIRST DEEP BREATH IN YEARS
BORN AGAIN

TO FEEL *anything* AT ALL

FROM VENUS TO MARS

PLEASE, MY DARLING, PULL YOUR TRUST FROM THE MOON—
EVEN SHE'S FULL OF INCONSISTENCY.
I DARE TO WISH INSTEAD THAT ONE DAY SOON
YOU MIGHT ENTRUST YOUR PRECIOUS FAITH IN ME.
BEFORE YOUR EYES, I DESPERATELY STAND
WITH A HOPEFUL HOLE GOUGED OUT FROM MY CHEST
AND THIS BEATING HEART THAT BLEEDS IN MY HANDS
TO PROVE TO YOU I'M NOT LIKE ALL THE REST
WHO EACH CAME IN INNOCENT LOVE'S DISGUISE
TO SPURN YOUR SPIRIT AND TO STEAL YOUR YOUTH.
LOOK HERE, THERE IS NO MASK BEFORE MY EYES.
I BEG YOU LISTEN AS I SING MY TRUTH,

AS LONG AS SUMMER BURNS AND EARTH ENDURES
UNTIL THE STARS FLEE THE NIGHT I AM YOURS.

r.clift

FROM MARS TO VENUS

ONCE MORE, LIKE THE SEARING FLESH OF THE SUN
MY SKIN BURNS AND BLISTERS WITHOUT YOUR TOUCH.
ALL WILL SUFFER UNTIL YOUR LIPS I'VE WON,
THIS I HAVE SWORN TO PROVE MYSELF ENOUGH.
I WILL ADORN YOUR BED WITH BONES OF GODS
CARVE OUT SINFUL SOULS OF THOSE UNWORTHY
AND PEEL THE VEINS FROM YOUR PAST LOVERS FLAWED,
FOR ONE WHO SCORNS YOU DESERVES NO MERCY.
MEET ME, I BEG YOU, STEAL INTO THE NIGHT
TO YOUR WILD BEAUTY I WISH TO SUCCUMB
COVER ME LIKE SOFT RAYS OF RAW MOONLIGHT
TELL ME WHEN, WHERE, HOW YOU CRAVE TO BE LOVED.

TILL THEN I'LL SPREAD ONLY CARNAGE AND GORE,
FOR YOUR HEART, I WILL RAGE A THOUSAND WARS.

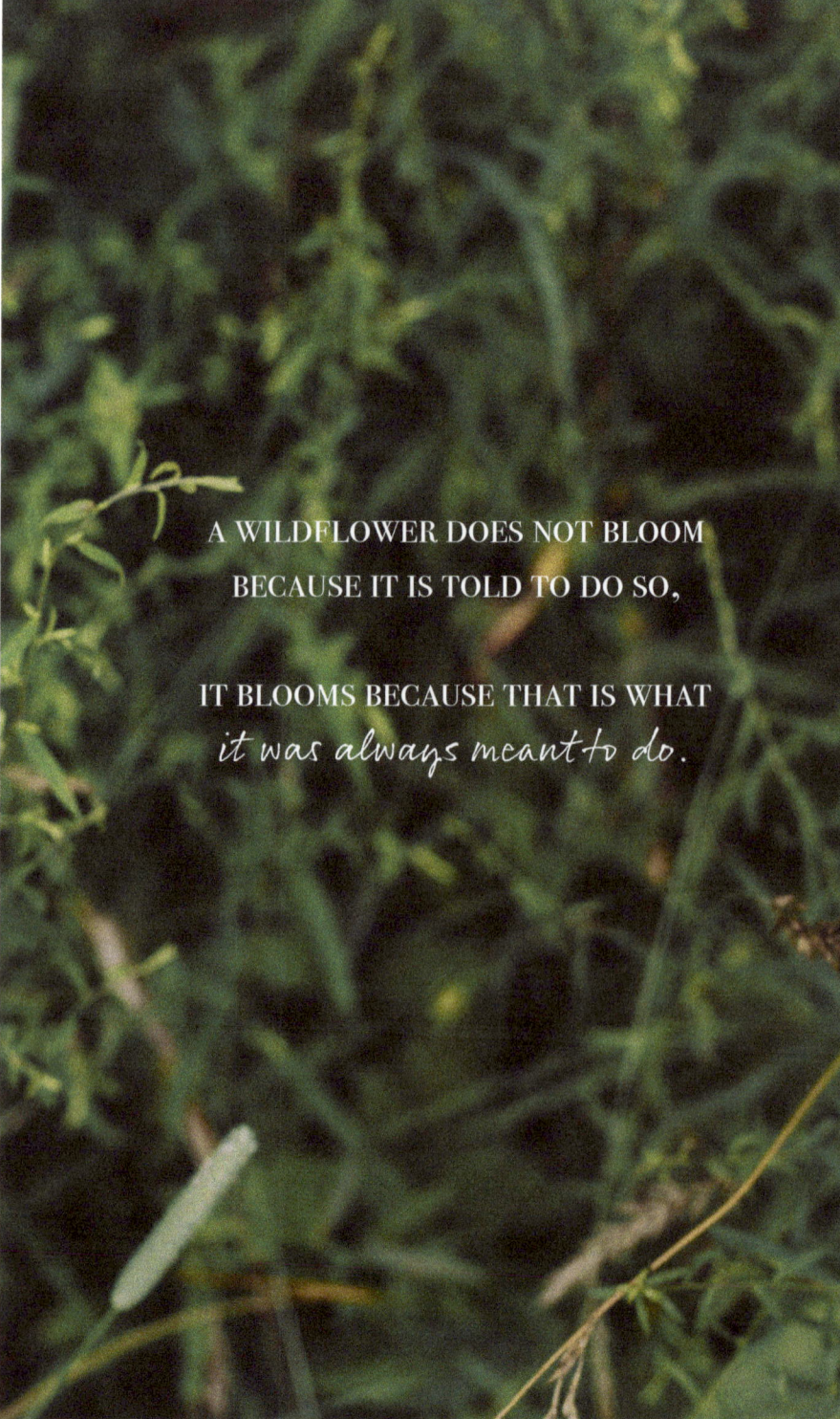

A WILDFLOWER DOES NOT BLOOM
BECAUSE IT IS TOLD TO DO SO,

IT BLOOMS BECAUSE THAT IS WHAT
it was always meant to do.

TO FEEL *anything* AT ALL

DO YOU REMEMBER WHEN YOU WERE YOUNG
AND HOW YOU WOULD CLIMB TREES
WITHOUT A THOUGHT OF HOW
TO GET BACK DOWN

UP AND UP AND UP
AS FAST AS YOU COULD

WIND BLOWING
HEART PULSING
HANDS SHAKING
TO TOUCH THE CLOUDS

SUNLIGHT WOULD PIERCE THROUGH
THE LEAVES AS YOU EMERGE FROM THE TOP
AND GET LOST IN THE VAST BEAUTY OF THE SKY

THEN YOU'D HEAR A VOICE CALL YOUR NAME
FROM THE GROUND AND SUDDENLY REALIZE
how far you could fall

THAT'S WHAT IT FEELS LIKE
LOVING YOU

HAVE YOU EVER MET SOMEONE
and after one honest conversation,
SUDDENLY, IT'S LIKE THEIR
EYES ARE SEEING STRAIGHT THROUGH
TO YOUR BARE SOUL,
AND YOU CAN'T HELP BUT WONDER—

WHERE

HAVE

YOU

BEEN?

TO FEEL *anything* AT ALL

TWO RESTLESS HANDS
FIDGETING AND TAPPING
SEARCHING FOR SOMETHING

HE PUTS HIS ON THE TABLE
AND SHE KEEPS HERS IN HER LAP

WHEN ALL THEY ~~WANT~~ NEED TO DO
IS HOLD EACH OTHER

for even as time may pass
AND THE SEARCH GOES ON—

THOSE TWO HANDS, TWO HEARTS BEATING,
SHOULD ALWAYS HAVE A CHANCE TO
FIND THEIR WAY BACK
WHEN THEY NEED TO REMEMBER
HOW IT FEELS TO BE LOVED

THAT'S THE THING ABOUT WINTER—
I'VE BEEN IN THE BITTER COLD
for so long
I CAN HARDLY RECALL WHAT IT WAS EVER LIKE
TO FEEL THE SUN BURN ON MY SKIN—
I'VE GOTTEN SO USED TO THE EMPTINESS
THE BARE OUTLOOK, THE ALONE,
I CAN'T FEEL IT ANY MORE. I'M NUMB.
MAYBE GOING NUMB IS EASIER
THAN FEELING COLD— THAN FEELING
THE ICY WIND BLOW AGAINST
MY BARE CHEST EVERY WAKING MOMENT
OF THE DAY

AFTER SO MUCH OF THAT— WHY EVEN OPEN
MY EYES AT ALL IF THEY'RE ONLY
GOING TO WATER AND STING
IN THE MORNING?
WHY EVEN BOTHER LETTING MY HEART
OUT OF ITS RIB CAGE IF IT'S ONLY
GOING TO COME BACK FROZEN SOLID AND
SHATTERED?

AND THEN YOU CAME ALONG
LIKE A DEEP BREATH OF FRESH AIR
AND I NEVER THOUGHT SPRING WOULD
COME AGAIN UNTIL YOUR SMILE
BLOSSOMED FLOWERS IN MY CHEST,
I THOUGHT BUTTERFLIES WERE EXTINCT
UNTIL YOU LOOKED AT ME—
YOUR EYES MAKE ME BELIEVE IN
HAZY SUNRISES AND BRIGHT BLUE SKIES,
YOUR TOUCH IS THE FIRST BIT OF WARMTH
I'VE FELT IN MONTHS
AND YOUR VOICE MAKES ME BELIEVE
THAT MAYBE THIS HEART STILL BEATS
FOR A REASON AND MAYBE I CAN
feel something more than nothing.

THAT MAYBE I AM CAPABLE OF LOVING AGAIN,
OF LIGHT, OF GROWTH, OF MORE
THAN JUST FADING AWAY—
I THINK WHAT I'M TRYING TO SAY IS
YOU MAKE ME BELIEVE IN SUMMER.

TO FEEL *anything* AT ALL

HERE I GAZE UP AT THE SKY

AND CLAIM THAT I LOVE THE STARS

BUT I DO NOT KNOW THEIR NAMES

r.clift

ALL MY HANDS HAVE
ARE EACH OTHER
AND THAT'S NOT ENOUGH
TO KEEP THEM WARM

i have this lovely idea
that instead of beating
my heart spins
like the needle of a compass

r.clift

THE ONLY WAY TO START
TRUSTING PEOPLE AGAIN
IS   TO   START
TRUSTING PEOPLE AGAIN

TO FEEL *anything* AT ALL

PICTURE HIS EYES,
THAT'S WHAT YOU FELL FOR FIRST, WASN'T IT?

NOW HIS SMILE. NOT THE FAKE ONE
IN PHOTOS BUT THE ONE JUST FOR YOU
THE ONE YOU FEEL WHILE KISSING HIM
THE ONE THAT MAKES YOU WEAK

HE SAYS YOUR NAME, IT'S DIFFERENT
FROM ANYONE ELSE— THE WAY IT COMES
FROM HIS LIPS. IT FILLS YOU WITH WARMTH

THE MAN YOU'RE THINKING OF, THE ONE
I JUST DESCRIBED. I HOPE YOU HAVE THE COURAGE
TO LOVE HIM
and if you don't
I HOPE ONE DAY YOU WILL

r.clift

I'D LIKE TO THINK

THAT THE TWINKLING

OF THE NIGHT SKY

IS THE STARS BREATHING

AS THEY SING TO EACH OTHER

THROUGH THE LONELINESS OF SPACE,

DESPITE ALL THEIR VOICES

BEING LOST IN THE VOID.

TO FEEL *anything* AT ALL

LIKE A WILTING FLOWER,
I ACHE FOR SUNLIGHT.
SELFISH CLOUDS HAVE KEPT HIM
HIDDEN ALL WEEK,
CASTING A BITTER SHADOW
OVER THE DAY. IS THE SKY
PUNISHING US? BUT FOR WHAT?
THE NIGHT IS TOO NEW TO
DWELL ON THAT NOW.

THE STARS ARE FIGHTING TO SHINE,
BUT NO LIGHT CAN BE SEEN.
MAYBE
THEY ALL LEFT.
IT'S FAR TOO COLD
TO BE OUT RIGHT NOW.
it's even too cold
FOR ANGELS TO FLY.
EVERYTHING FEELS
FROZEN— ESPECIALLY ME.
FROM THE INSIDE OUT.

r.clift

THE ENDLESS RAIN
PATTERS OUTSIDE MY WINDOW,
A SINGLE LAMP ILLUMINATES
A TINY CORNER OF THE ROOM—

THE CHILL MOVES SLOWLY
THROUGH THE AIR TO ABIDE
A KIND OF STILLNESS THAT
can only be found in november—
AFTER ALL THE LEAVES HAVE
FALLEN AND WE'VE SETTLED
INTO OUR BEDS
TO MAKE IT THROUGH
THE WINTER.

MY HEART BEATS
FOR NO ONE.

r.clift

DO NOT FOOL YOURSELF
INTO COMING ANY CLOSER

THOSE WHO LOOK AT ME
with eyes like that
END UP GETTING SMOTHERED

AND I AM TIRED OF BEING
THE MONSTER

TO FEEL *anything* AT ALL

THERE ARE CORPSES THAT WALK AMONG
THE LIVING DAY TO DAY
WAKING UP WITH THE SUNRISE, GOING TO WORK,
READING A BOOK, STUDYING FOR TESTS, REPAIRING
A BROKEN LOCK, STUCK ON THE SIDE OF THE ROAD,
CLIMBING A MOUNTAIN
THEY LOOK JUST LIKE YOU AND ME,
BUT THE DIFFERENCE IS— THEY'RE NUMB
UNFEELING
THEY'VE TURNED IT ALL OFF
EITHER ON PURPOSE, OR BY ACCIDENT
IT ALL JUST BECAME TOO MUCH
TO BE WORTH IT
i know because i used to be one of them
DULLED TO MY SURROUNDINGS,
LIKE A LANTERN WITHOUT A FLAME—
EMPTY. COLD.
TRUST ME WHEN I SAY, IT IS BETTER
TO FEEL PAIN THAN TO FEEL NOTHING AT ALL
BECAUSE AT LEAST WHEN YOUR HEART
FEELS LIKE IT HAS SHATTERED, WHEN
YOU CAN'T CRY ANOTHER TEAR WITHOUT
PASSING OUT, AND YOUR HEAD IS POUNDING BEYOND
BELIEF— AT LEAST WHEN YOU FEEL
THAT KIND OF PAIN—
YOU FEEL ALIVE.

AND NOW, EVEN FROM
HALFWAY ACROSS
THE WORLD AND
NO WORDS SPOKEN
BETWEEN US—
I NEED YOU TO KNOW
it is possible to love
IN SILENCE

she was finally out of the dark
alive to see the dawn

but with the sun
in her eyes
HE WAS GONE

I KNOW YOU DON'T BELIEVE ME
BUT THIS HURT YOU'RE FEELING
CAN BE BEAUTIFUL—
IN THIS SPECTRUM OF
being human
THE DARKNESS BETWEEN
THE STARS IS JUST AS
IMPORTANT AS THE LIGHT

r.clift

BRAVE GIRL, THERE IS NO MORE TIME TO HIDE,
THE DRUMS ARE POUNDING, CALLING US,
FOR WE MUST STAND AND FIGHT--
TO BE HEARD, TO BE SEEN,
to be unapologetically woman.

I SEE THE FEAR
IN YOUR CORNFLOWER EYES,
AND WATCH THEM CAST TO THE GROUND--
HIDING THE HUMILIATION YOU FEEL
AS YOU TIE A COAT AROUND YOUR WAIST
AND ONCE AGAIN, ACHE TO RUN AWAY.

THE CONSTANT PAIN THAT PULSES
THROUGH YOUR BODY IS NOTHING
COMPARED TO THE CRUELNESS THROWN AT YOU
FROM THOSE WHO DON'T UNDERSTAND
THAT YOU ARE A MIRACLE--

DON'T YOU SEE?
NOT ONLY CAN YOU CREATE LIFE WITHIN YOU,
BUT YOU WERE MADE WITH
THE HEART TO NURTURE IT
AND STRENGTH TO PROTECT IT.

YOU, BRAVE GIRL,
ARE A WARRIOR
AND WARRIORS ARE
NEVER ASHAMED TO BLEED.

SOMEWHERE DEEP IN THE COUNTRYSIDE

WHERE THE SUN LAYS DOWN TO SLEEP

she feels his touch trickle over her skin

AS HE WHISPERS HER NAME

WITH A VOICE THAT COULD SWOON THE MOON

TO FEEL *anything* AT ALL

**LOOK AT HOW SHE FLOATS
ACROSS THE ROOM WITHOUT
A CARE IN THE WORLD**

*someone had too much
to dream last night*

r.clift

IT IS THE KINDNESS OF YOUR SOUL
AND THE LOVE WITHIN YOUR HEART
THAT MATTER ABOVE ALL ELSE

*i would do my best
to remember that*

THEY CALLED ME SIREN, AND FOR THE
LONGEST TIME I HID BEHIND
METAPHOR AND SHADOW, CLOSED EYES
AND SILENCE, FOR THEIR DROWNING
WAS MY FAULT. I WAS ALWAYS TOLD
IT WAS MY FAULT.
UNTIL THE MOMENT I, MYSELF
HEARD A SIREN SONG—
AN UNAPOLOGETIC VOICE CLAIMING
THE AIR AROUND HER AS HER OWN,
CALLING TO EVERYTHING OR NOTHING
OR JUST THE SEA ITSELF—
FOR WHEN I ASKED HER
WHO SHE SANG FOR
SHE TOLD ME SHE SANG
FOR NO ONE BUT HERSELF,

SHE TOLD ME IF THEY LISTEN AND THEY FALL
AND IF THEY ARE TOO FOOLISH NOT TO
HOLD OUT THEIR ARMS AND SWIM
THEN IT IS THEIR FAULT FOR CHOOSING NOT
TO KEEP THEIR OWN HEAD ABOVE WATER.
your voice is not theirs to silence,
SHE TOLD ME—
AND FINALLY I BELIEVED IT.

r.clift

THE MORE I USE MY NEWFOUND
VOICE TO TOUCH THE
INNER PARTS OF PEOPLE
THAT ARE RARELY NOTICED, CARED FOR,
OR SPOKEN TO— THE MORE I AM CONVINCED
THAT THIS IS THE VERY REASON I HAVE
A VOICE IN THE FIRST PLACE.

IF I'M GOING TO SAY ANYTHING,
i want it to be felt.
I'VE SPENT TOO MUCH OF MY LIFE
BEING QUIETLY IGNORED— NOW
IS MY TIME TO SAY SOMETHING,
TO SPEAK TO THE HEARTS THAT NEED IT
AND ASSURE THEM— THEY ARE
NOT ALONE. I'M NOT GIVING UP
UNTIL EVERYONE HAS FELT
MY WORDS.
I WILL BE
REMEMBERED.

TO FEEL *anything* AT ALL

HE WAS MY ANGEL WITH DIRTY WINGS,
COMING DOWN FROM THE STARS AND
CALLING ME WITH HIS WORDS
LIKE NO ONE EVER HAS BEFORE—

WE BEWITCHED EACH OTHER WITH
LIPS AND HANDS LIKE A STRANGE MAGIC.

HE TASTED OF CIGARETTE SMOKE AND
CHEAP WINE— OF WHICH I COULD NOT HAVE
ENOUGH.

A VOICE IN MY HEAD REMINDED ME
He is not yours to keep.
BUT THAT DID NOT STOP ME FROM
HOLDING ON.

IN THE END THOUGH, NO MATTER HOW
TIGHTLY I GRIPPED HIS HANDS,
HE FLEW AWAY— AND I
AM STILL ON THE GROUND,
LOOKING UP.

r.clift

I NEED YOU
TO TOUCH ME
G E N T L Y
LIKE THE MOONLIGHT
SPILLING IN FROM MY WINDOW

AND COVER ME WITH
W A R M T H
LIKE AN EXTRA BLANKET
IN WINTER

AND THEN
M A Y B E
I CAN SLEEP THROUGH THE NIGHT

TO FEEL *anything* AT ALL

NEXT TIME, SHE NEEDS TO BE KISSED BY SOMEONE WHO KNOWS WHAT THE HELL HE IS DOING—

WHO WHISPERS IN HER EAR, MAKES HER FEEL W A N T E D AND MOST IMPORTANTLY— KNOWS WHAT TO DO WITH HIS HANDS

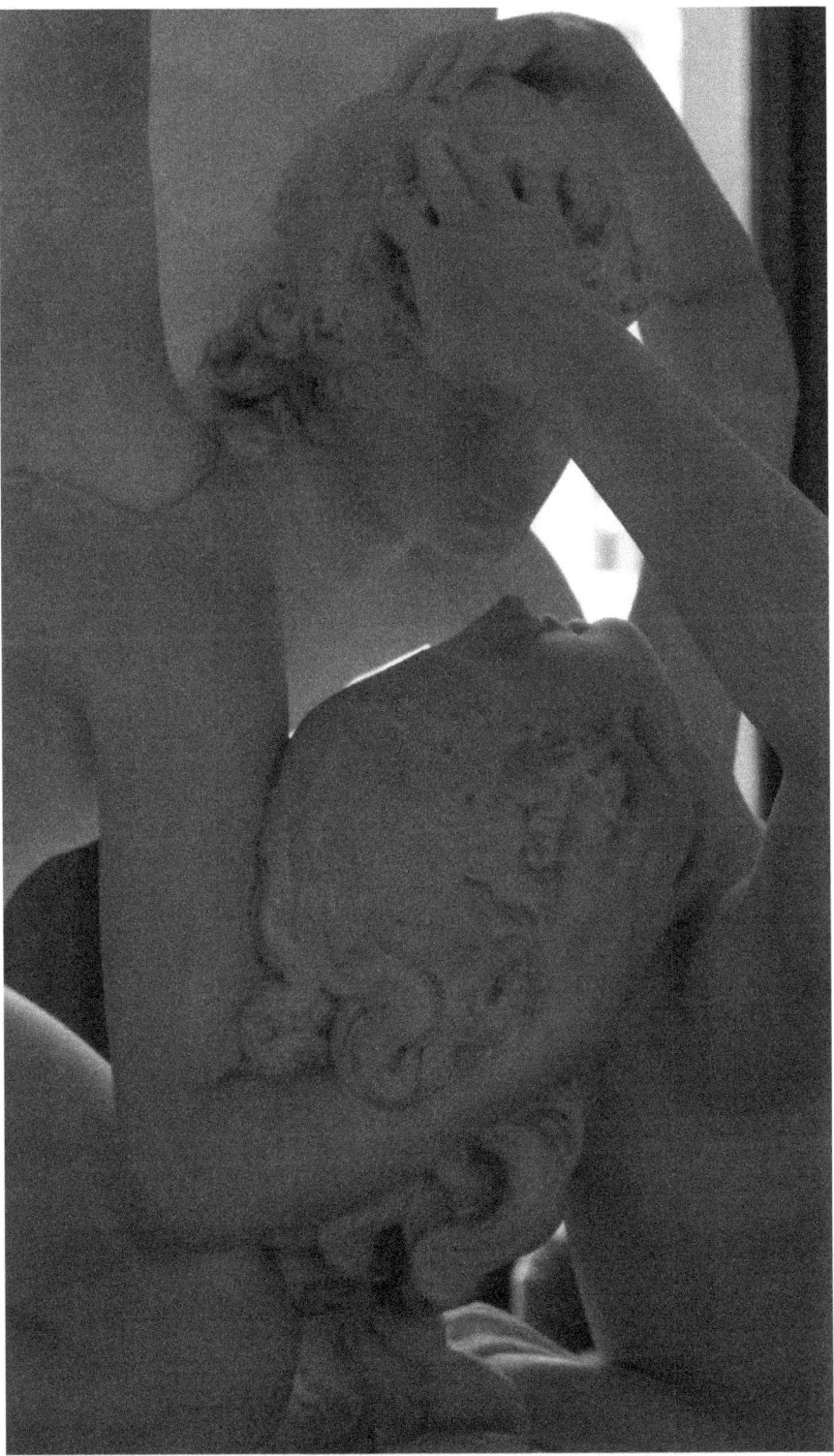

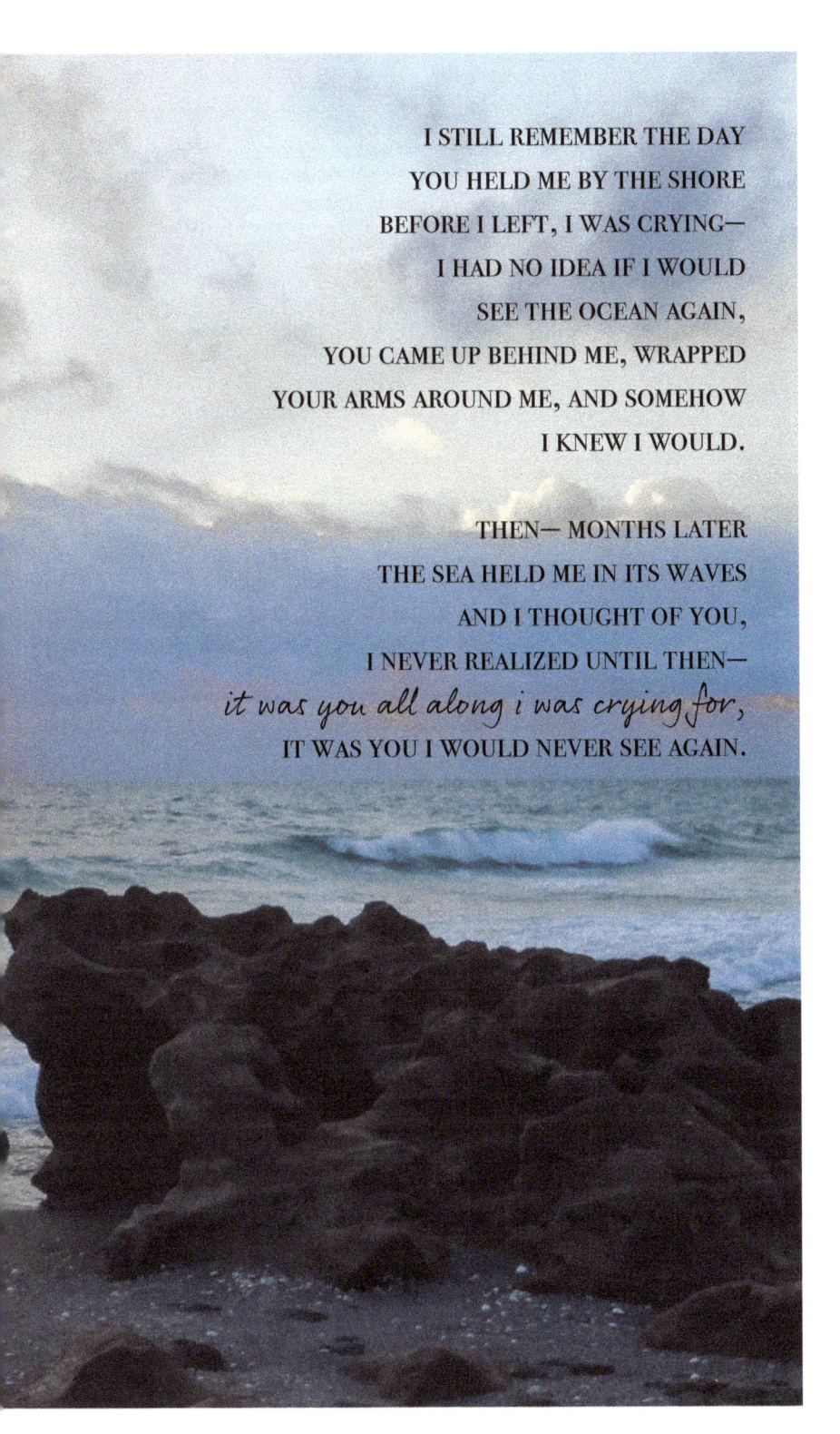

I STILL REMEMBER THE DAY
YOU HELD ME BY THE SHORE
BEFORE I LEFT, I WAS CRYING—
I HAD NO IDEA IF I WOULD
SEE THE OCEAN AGAIN,
YOU CAME UP BEHIND ME, WRAPPED
YOUR ARMS AROUND ME, AND SOMEHOW
I KNEW I WOULD.

THEN— MONTHS LATER
THE SEA HELD ME IN ITS WAVES
AND I THOUGHT OF YOU,
I NEVER REALIZED UNTIL THEN—
it was you all along i was crying for,
IT WAS YOU I WOULD NEVER SEE AGAIN.

TO FEEL *anything* AT ALL

THE LOVE I FEEL FOR YOU
NEVER REALLY DISAPPEARED.
IT MAY NOT BE THE
ROARING WILDFIRE IT ONCE WAS,
BUT THESE TENDER EMBERS
HAVE SINCE BURNED IN MY HEART—
SILENT, INTIMATE, NEVER
GOING COLD, NOT COMPLETELY.

I THOUGHT I WAS SUPPOSED
TO SNUFF THEM OUT BUT
NOTHING WORKED,
THEN I REALIZED,
THOSE EMBERS—
they're all that's left of you
TO KEEP ME WARM.

r.clift

I KEEP TRYING
TO TELL MYSELF
IT'S OKAY THAT YOU LEFT.
IT'S OKAY, THAT I DON'T KNOW
WHAT LOVE FEELS LIKE
ANYMORE.
THAT SOMEHOW, I'M BETTER OFF.
WHY FEEL LOVE WHEN
YOU HAVE NO ONE
TO SHARE IT WITH?
TO GIVE IT TO? TO LOVE YOU BACK?

IT WOULD JUST BE BEST TO FORGET,
TO PRETEND IT NEVER HAPPENED,
BACK WHEN I DIDN'T EVEN
KNOW WHAT I WAS MISSING—
but i've tried. i can't forget.
NOW THAT I KNOW THE TRUTH,
NOTHING ELSE MATTERS.
FOR WHO WOULD SEE COLOR
AND THEN WANT TO GO BACK
TO A WORLD OF GREY?

TO FEEL *anything* AT ALL

SHE PLACED HER HAND
ON HIS HEART AND
IT AWOKE GENTLY
TO THE WORDS FROM
HER LIPS
it's time to love again

r.clift

IT WAS DIFFERENT—
hearing you say my name
COMPARED TO ANYONE ELSE.

YOU WEREN'T JUST ASKING
FOR MY ATTENTION
OR GREETING ME AT THE DOOR,

YOU WERE CALLING FOR
MY SOUL
AND IT LISTENED.

TO FEEL *anything* AT ALL

I'M LIKE A TIMID FIREFLY
ON A HAZY SUMMER EVENING

AND YOU AN EAGER YOUNG BOY
WITH AN EMPTY JAR

I DART AND GLOW AND TEASE
beckoning you to chase me
BUT ABSOLUTELY TERRIFIED
OF BEING TRAPPED

r.clift

SOMEDAY
SOMEONE
WILL LOVE YOU FOR
YOUR SPIRIT
FOR YOUR LIGHT HEART
AND HEAVY PASSION,
FOR YOUR FEARLESS VULNERABILITY
AND OVERWHELMING INSECURITIES,
FOR THE CRINKLES BESIDE
YOUR EYES WHEN YOU LAUGH

*but my darling
i'm sorry*
THAT SOMEONE
ISN'T ME

SHE SEES THE BEST
IN EVERYONE
AND IT WILL BE
her most welcome
UNDOING

SOME GIRLS ARE WILDFIRES
BUT SHE'S FAR TOO
SUBTLE FOR THAT

IMAGINE A GLOWING EMBER
SILENTLY BURNING
persisting

EVEN AFTER ALL THE OTHER FLAMES
HAVE GONE OUT

TO FEEL anything AT ALL

I THREW OPEN THE WIRE DOOR
BUT THE LITTLE BIRD DIDN'T FLY OUT

SHE DIDN'T EVEN APPROACH THE OPENING

DOES SHE WISH TO BE FREE?
does she know that she isn't?

I DON'T UNDERSTAND HOW A CAGED BIRD
STILL HAS THE WILL TO SING
WHILE IMPRISONED

BUT MAYBE
IT'S NOT A SONG AT ALL
MAYBE SHE'S CRYING

AND ALL WE HEAR IS MUSIC

r.clift

I THINK ABOUT THE NIGHT YOU LEFT AND HOW

if it had been a movie

YOU WOULD'VE LOOKED BACK AT ME

THROUGH THE RAINY WINDOW OR

I WOULD'VE CHASED YOU OUTSIDE

WITH ARMS WIDE OPEN

BUT IT WASN'T A MOVIE

YOU DIDN'T LOOK BACK

AND I STAYED INSIDE

TO FEEL *anything* AT ALL

ISN'T IT WONDERFUL, HOW IN A MOMENT
just a moment
OF LOOKING AT EACH OTHER IN
THE RIGHT WAY—
WE CAN LIVE A LIFETIME
IN EACH OTHER'S EYES,

UNTIL SOMEONE BLINKS

TIME IS UP

AND WE HAVE TO SAY
GOODBYE

r.clift

DREAMS WERE MADE FOR LOVERS LIKE
YOU AND ME, SEPARATED
BY UNFORTUNATE CIRCUMSTANCE

SO AFTER EVERY ACHING DAY
AS WE LIVE OUR LIVES APART,
A NIGHT IS SPENT HOLDING EACH OTHER,

BECAUSE WHEN SLEEP TAKES ME,
you're there
I FEEL YOUR ARMS AROUND ME—
THE ARMS I'VE WAITED FOR ALL DAY,
THE UNIVERSE SMILES
AND WE ARE FINALLY,
FOR FAR TOO LITTLE TIME
TOGETHER

your kiss was not without consequence —
MY EARS RANG,
MY HANDS SHOOK,
AND A CHILL CRAWLED AROUND
IN MY SKIN.

I FELT AS IF
MY FEET WERE NUMB
AND I WASN'T SURE
IF I WOULD FALL TO THE GROUND
OR FLOAT AWAY.

TO FEEL *anything* AT ALL

there is a certain part of me
that comes alive
just to die
for those that don't
want me back

I THINK WHAT I'M TRYING TO SAY IS—
I KNEW I WAS DISAPPOINTING YOU WHEN I
FINALLY FLEW AWAY

OUT OF REACH

r.clift

OUR LOVE WAS BEAUTIFULLY SHORT LIVED
LIKE THE SETTING SUMMER SUN
but i never got quite close enough
TO HOLD ONTO YOU FOR LONG

ALTHOUGH WE FOUND OUR LIPS
TOGETHER
YOUR HEART WAS CAREFULLY
WITHHELD
AND LIKE WIND SLIPPING
THROUGH MY FINGERS
YOU WERE GONE
BEFORE AUTUMN FELL

TO FEEL *anything* AT ALL

THERE IS A CERTAIN KIND OF TRANQUILITY
IN AN EMPTY THEATRE

THE AIR IS STILL
AND THE HOUSE IS QUIET

THE STAGE FROZEN IN TIME

THE ONLY SOUND IS THE BUILDING SETTLING,
TRYING TO GET COMFORTABLE

THE GHOST LIGHT STANDS CENTER STAGE
TO BRIGHTEN THE DARKNESS OF THE ROOM

IT'S A PLACE I LIKE TO VISIT
on my own
TO SHARE IN ITS SERENE CALMNESS

WHO KNEW, EVEN WITHOUT A SCRIPT—
THE STAGE CAN OFFER AN ESCAPE,

AFTER ALL, ISN'T THAT WHAT THEATRE
WAS ALWAYS MEANT TO DO?

TO TAKE PEOPLE AWAY FROM THEIR WORRIES,
EVEN IF FOR ONLY A MOMENT.

TO FEEL *anything* AT ALL

WE MUST HAVE BEEN MADE
FROM THE SAME BREATH
OF THE UNIVERSE

*because when i saw you
for the first time*

THE STARDUST REBORN
IN OUR SOULS
RECOGNIZED EACH OTHER

AND THAT IS WHY
IT FEELS LIKE I HAVE KNOWN YOU
ALL ALONG

r.clift

I HOPE, IF THERE IS EVER
A NEXT TIME
I'LL FALL FOR A WRITER
OR AT LEAST
A LOVER OF WORDS

SOMEONE WHO CAN SPEAK
TO THE PART OF ME
only poetry
CAN REACH

r.clift

I'M TERRIFIED
THAT ONE DAY
I'LL SEE YOU AGAIN

AND YOU'LL BE
IN THE ARMS
OF SOMEONE ELSE

LIKE THE WARM RAYS
OF THE SUN

*i can feel your touch
burn in my skin*

FROM MILES
AND MILES AWAY

I THINK THE MOMENT
YOU REALLY GROW UP
IS THE MOMENT YOU REALIZE
not everyone you love
IS GOING TO LOVE YOU BACK

IF YOU WANT TO SEE LIVING ART
IN FRONT OF YOUR EYES
PAY ATTENTION
AS A POET CRIES—
they have a way
OF MAKING PAIN
FEEL BEAUTIFUL

TO FEEL *anything* AT ALL

IT WAS ONCE MY FAVORITE SONG,
THE BEAT OF OUR HEARTS TOGETHER,
HARMONIOUS AS THE SUMMER EVENING SKY—
BUT NOW THIS CONSTANT POUNDING
OF A SINGLE HEART
IS DEAFENING IN AN EMPTY ROOM.

The music is lost forever, and so are you.

r.clift

I'M AFRAID TO ASK
IF YOU'RE STILL
IN LOVE WITH ME

AND I THINK
IT'S BECAUSE
I ALREADY KNOW
THE ANSWER

TO FEEL *anything* AT ALL

IT'S SOMETHING
IN THE EYES— BROWN EYES
ARE STABLE, LIKE SOLID GROUND—
SOMEWHERE TO
LIE DOWN AND REST.
BREATHE. TRUST. SOFT EARTH
TO PLANT ROOTS AND GROW.

BUT BLUE EYES— THOSE ADRIFT BLUE
EYES ARE DECEPTIVE, TREACHEROUSLY
DEEP. I ALWAYS SEEM
TO GET LOST AT SEA— AND AT FIRST
THAT MYSTERIOUS DEPTH IS
CAPTIVATING, EXCITING, ENGULFING,
but in the end
I DROWN

r.clift

WHY DO WE
ALWAYS SEEK
ABSOLUTION?
WHEN I SWAM
ACROSS THE OCEAN
TO FIND
YOUR MEMORY—
INTO THE SEASIDE
INTO THE OPEN REACHES
sinking
WHAT DO YOU
DO WITH THE PIECES
OF A BROKEN
HEART?
WE ONCE STOOD
STEADY AS THE
STARS— I CAN SEE
IT IN YOUR EYES—
YOU
WILL ALWAYS BE
DANGEROUS

i'm not playing hard to get
because i'm not playing
my heart does not like games
and my body is not a prize

TO FEEL *anything* AT ALL

I'M BEGGING YOU TO GIVE UP
NOT BECAUSE I BELIEVE YOU LACK
THE HEART FOR IT, OR BECAUSE
YOU DON'T HAVE THE STRENGTH,
BUT TURN AROUND AND LOOK, MY DEAR,

you cannot fly without wings

r.clift

WHATEVER YOU DO
MY DEAR ONE
*do it with all the love
in your heart*
FOR A LIFE IS NEVER TRULY
LIVED
IF ONE IS TO LIVE A LIFE
WITHOUT LOVE

r.clift

HE'S MADE OF A THOUSAND WORDS
THAT PLAGUE HIM—

ESCAPING ONLY THROUGH HIS
FINGERTIPS ON THE WORN OUT KEYS
OF AN OLD TYPEWRITER

OF DESIRES THAT PULL HIM
TO THE OTHER SIDE OF THE GLOBE
WHILE HIS FEET STAY UNWILLINGLY
ROOTED TO THE EARTH BELOW HIM

AND OF EYES— EYES THAT READ
THE WORDS STIRRING BEHIND MINE
AND LOOK AT ME IN A WAY
I NEVER KNEW
I WANTED TO BE LOOKED AT

TO FEEL *anything* AT ALL

IT DOESN'T MATTER IF YOU COVER
YOURSELF IN SAPPHIRES AND RUBIES
BECAUSE WHAT'S UNDERNEATH YOUR SKIN

*isn't so easy to understand
as gems in just the right
configuration, but stricken*

AS THE LIGHT THAT PIERCES THROUGH
A DIAMOND AND BREAKS ITSELF
INTO SHARDS ACROSS THE WALL
TO REMIND YOU THAT BROKEN
CAN BE BEAUTIFUL—

*a jewel in many parts fractured
but whole*

TO FEEL *anything* AT ALL

HOW CAN YOU EXPECT ME
TO KEEP MY FEET
ON THE GROUND
WHEN YOU ARE FULLY AWARE
THAT I CAN FLY?
FOR NOW I MAY WALK BESIDE YOU,
BUT YOU SHOULD KNOW THIS WON'T LAST
FOREVER.
i love you, i will always love you,
BUT WHEN THE STARS CALL—
I MUST GO.

I WILL ALWAYS
CHOOSE MY WINGS.

r.clift

YOU SPEND YOUR NIGHTS
STARING AT THE STARS
WAITING FOR ONE TO FALL

BUT DON'T YOU KNOW
*they're safe
and happy there*

AND DON'T YOU KNOW
YOU CANNOT HOLD A STAR
IN YOUR MORTAL HANDS

DON'T YOU KNOW?

SO WHY
DO YOU
STILL WISH
FOR STARS
TO FALL

TO FEEL *anything* AT ALL

YESTERDAY, SHE BURNED.

SHE CRIED OUT IN CRACKLING
FLAMES, EMBER, SMOKE,
THE FALL OF HER OUTSTRETCHED HAND TO HEAVEN
SOUNDED LIKE A HUNDRED YEARS OF PRAYER COLLAPSING
AS THE INFERNO ENGULFED HER FROM THE INSIDE OUT

SHE QUESTIONED HER SALVATION,
HER TEAR STAINED GLASS WINDOWS
GLOWED AFRAID AND ABLAZE
AS THE SUN HID BEHIND THE HORIZON—
NO LONGER ABLE TO BEAR WITNESS TO HER PAIN,
LEAVING HER DEVASTATION TO CARRY INTO THE NIGHT
WITH NO END IN SIGHT—

BUT TODAY—
DAWN BREAKS LIKE A THOUSAND GENTLE VOICES
WHISPERING HER FAITH,
A REVERENT SILENCE DANCES THROUGH
HER OPEN WOUNDS
CARRYING ALL THE HOPE IN THE WORLD
all the hope in the world
AND AS DEWY EYES BLINK AWAKE
A SOFT MORNING LIGHT SHINES PAST SMOLDERING ASH
THROUGH ROSE WINDOWS UNBROKEN
TO REVEAL A HEART OF TENDER STONE—
A HEART THAT ENDURED.

AS THE SUN RISES AGAIN,
SO WILL OUR LADY.

r.clift

WE ARE IMMORTAL. EVERLASTING.
IMPRISONED IN MARBLE,
HELD CAPTIVE BY LOVE,
PERPETUALLY IN EACH OTHER'S ARMS.

TOGETHER IN PARIS OUR PASSION
IS SEEN AS TIMELESS.

Desire fills the space between us.

FOR CENTURIES WE HAVE BEEN CONFINED
IN TENDER STONE, LOCKED IN MID-EMBRACE,
LONGING TO SHARE A KISS,

BUT THE SCULPTOR WAS CRUEL
CARVING US TO BE
FOREVER SO CLOSE,

BUT NEVER CLOSE ENOUGH.

TO FEEL *anything* AT ALL

AT FIRST, WHEN YOU SAY GOODBYE
TO THE LOVE OF YOUR LIFE
IT HURTS
IT HURTS LIKE HELL
AND EVERY MOMENT YOU MISS THEM,
THE HURT COMES BACK.

BUT IF YOU GIVE IT SOME TIME
maybe more than you think
YOU'LL BEGIN TO SMILE EACH TIME
YOU MISS THEM
BECAUSE EACH TIME YOU MISS THEM,
YOU THINK OF THEM. AND THEIR SMILE.
AND THEIR LAUGH AND EMBRACE AND EYES AND
HOW THEY USED TO SAY YOUR NAME

so please
miss me
MISS ME EVERY HOUR
MISS ME EVERY MINUTE
MISS ME AND NEVER FORGET ME
NOT EVEN FOR A MOMENT

THEY SAY IF YOU LOVE SOMEONE LET THEM GO, BUT WHAT IF YOU KNOW THE MOMENT THEY LEAVE, YOU WILL SHATTER

ONE DAY, HE WILL BE ONLY WORDS.
POEMS WRITTEN. FEELINGS FELT.
AND ON THAT DAY, WHEN YOU FEEL
NOTHING AS YOU READ OF HIM—
THAT'S WHEN YOU'LL KNOW
you're free.

TO FEEL *anything* AT ALL

YOU SPARK AND SHINE
FROM THE INSIDE OUT
AND I AM JUST ANOTHER
FOOLISH MOTH TO THE FLAME,

INEXPLICABLY AND INESCAPABLY
DRAWN

EVEN THOUGH IT MEANS,
in the end,
BURNING.

r.clift

I OFTEN WONDER IF YOU MISSED ME.
IF YOU THOUGHT OF ME
IN THE DAYS AFTER YOU LEFT,
or did i fade quickly

LIKE A SAND CASTLE BEING
WASHED AWAY BY THE SEA—

HOW EASY AM I TO FORGET?

YOU'RE A THIEF
you steal from me each day
SMILES
BREATH
SLEEP
AND THE THOUGHTS THAT I
WAS MADE TO BE ALONE

ON THE NIGHTS WHEN YOU MISS ME
LIKE I KNOW YOU DO
LOOK UP AT THE MOON AND
TELL HER SO

SHE AND I ARE FRIENDS, YOU KNOW,
AND YOUR WORDS WILL MAKE IT TO ME

THEN IN THE MORNING
BEFORE THE STARS FADE INTO THE SUNLIGHT
listen

FOR THEY WILL WHISPER YOUR NAME
AND TELL YOU HOW I LOVE YOU STILL

PLEASE KNOW,
I ALWAYS WILL.

IF THERE IS MAGIC IN THIS WORLD
IT IS NOT IN ONLY YOU
OR ME,
but the space in between
AND THE LOVE THAT LIVES THERE

r.clift

MY GRANDMOTHER ONCE TOLD ME
SOME HONEY BEES
HAVE A FAVORITE FLOWER

A BELOVED BLOOM IT RETURNS TO
DAY AFTER DAY

OUT OF ALL THE THISTLES,
SWEETCLOVER, AND DANDELIONS
it favors only one

SHE ASSURED ME—
NO MATTER RAIN OR WIND
THAT HONEY BEE
WILL FIND A WAY TO ITS FLOWER

I COULDN'T MAKE SENSE OF WHY THE HONEY BEE
KEPT GOING BACK WHEN IT HAD A FIELD
OF FRESH BLOSSOMS TO CHOOSE FROM

I DIDN'T THINK IT MATTERED
UNTIL I MET YOU

TO FEEL *anything* AT ALL

I CAN'T GUARANTEE HOW YOU'LL FEEL
IN A DAY, THREE WEEKS,
OR FIVE MONTHS FROM NOW

BUT THE ONLY THING
that actually matters
IS THIS SECOND
AND THE NEXT
AND IF YOU'RE LUCKY
THE NEXT FEW MINUTES

BECAUSE RIGHT NOW
YOU FEEL SAFE,
RIGHT NOW
YOU FEEL HAPPINESS
WELLED UP IN YOUR CHEST,

AND YOU FEEL LOVED,

THAT'S WHY
I'M HOLDING YOUR HAND.

r.clift

WHAT I'M MOST AFRAID OF
IS THAT ONE DAY
YOU WILL LOOK AT ME
LIKE YOU LOOK AT A STRANGER—

WITH NO MORE LOVE IN YOUR EYES

TO FEEL *anything* AT ALL

EVEN ON THE BRIGHTEST SUMMER DAYS,
I FIND MYSELF IN DARKNESS—
LOST AMONG THE IN BETWEEN MOMENTS
CREEPING BENEATH MY SKIN IN SILENT
REMINISCENCE

THIS IS THE TIME
WHEN I REMEMBER HOW ALONE
I REALLY AM
HOW ALONE
I'LL ALWAYS BE

THIS IS THE TIME
WHEN I REMEMBER YOUR ARMS
AROUND ME—
BEING WITH YOU FELT LIKE
COMING IN FROM THE COLD.
it was like coming home.
I FEAR,
I'LL NEVER FEEL
AT HOME AGAIN.
NOT IN THIS BODY.
NOT WITHOUT YOU.

r.clift

I CATCH MY MIND
FROM TIME TO TIME
WANDERING BACK TO YOU—

IN THOSE MOMENTS
I RECALL YOUR TOUCH
AND THE WAY GOODBYE
ROLLED OFF YOUR TONGUE
FAR EASIER THAN I HAD HOPED.

IT WAS COMPLICATED, I KNOW,
IN THE FACT THAT WE WERE NEVER
MEANT TO LAST—

BUT UNTIL THE SUN GOES DARK
I WILL REMEMBER US
IN OUR LOVE THAT NEVER WAS
AND ALWAYS WILL BE.

TO FEEL *anything* AT ALL

DON'T CALL ME THE ONE
THAT GOT AWAY

THAT MAKES ME SOUND LIKE
A ONCE IN A LIFETIME
KIND OF PERSON

BUT I'M NOT, I'M NOTHING SPECIAL
I'M JUST A GIRL YOU ONCE KNEW
WHO MADE YOU FEEL SOMETHING
UNTIL ONE DAY

I LEFT
and never came back

r.clift

YOUR WARMTH
surrounded me
AND I DON'T RECALL
HAVING EVER FELT
MORE LOVED

*until i opened my eyes
to see the morning light*

AND AS YOUR ARMS FADED
INTO THE TIGHTLY WOUND SHEETS
I REALIZED
YOU WERE ONLY A DREAM

TO FEEL *anything* AT ALL

A STILL, MOONLESS NIGHT—
I LAY MY HEAD DOWN ON YOUR CHEST,
AND LISTEN TO YOUR HEART
BEAT
SLOW
AND YOUR BREATH STEADY
AS YOU DRIFT AWAY
A MOMENT OF SLEEP
THEN, OUT OF NOWHERE
YOU FLINCH
AWAKE
AND HOLD ONTO ME

WHEN I ASK IF YOU'RE OKAY
YOU NOD YOUR HEAD
AND TELL ME YOU FELT LIKE
you were falling
AND THE ONLY THING
I CAN THINK OF
WHILE LOOKING INTO
THOSE ENDLESS BROWN EYES
IS THE INESCAPABLE FEELING THAT
i am falling too

r.clift

I FIND MYSELF STARING AT THE
VASTNESS OF THE SKY—

UNTIL I REALIZE
GOD MADE ME LIMITED
AND I WAS NEVER MEANT TO FLY

TO FEEL *anything* AT ALL

HOLD ONTO THAT FIERCE HEART NOW,
TIGHTER THAN EVER.
DON'T LET THEM TAKE IT.

don't ever let them tame you,
WILD THING.

r.clift

YOU'RE THE ONE THAT POINTED OUT THAT I'M TOO STUBBORN.

THAT I'M INSATIABLY DETERMINED TO GET WHAT I WANT. SELFISH, EVEN. TO THE POINT OF TAKING SOMETHING THAT MIGHT NOT BE MINE TO TAKE. THAT I WON'T STOP UNTIL I CAN HOLD IN MY HANDS

WHAT I'VE SET MY MIND ON.

SO WHY ARE YOU SURPRISED WHEN I TAKE YOUR HAND, HOLD IT TIGHT AND KISS YOUR NECK, BECAUSE

ALL I WANT IS YOU.

HER EYES HOLD STARS,
HER CHEEKS BLOOM LIKE ROSES AND
HER LIPS CAN'T HELP BUT SMILE
EVERYTIME
SHE SAYS HIS NAME.

AS LONG AS THE SUN
AND MOON ENDURE
i am yours

TO FEEL *anything* AT ALL

IT'S MADDENING—
HEARING YOUR VOICE IN CROWDS
SEEING YOUR FACE ON STRANGERS
THINKING EACH TIME
it could actually be you

I STOP COLD
MY HEART DROPS
AND MY BREATH CATCHES
IN MY THROAT
UNTIL THE MIRAGE FADES AWAY
LEAVING ONLY THE MEMORY
OF THE DAY YOU LEFT

YOU ARE EVERYWHERE I LOOK
AND NOWHERE TO BE FOUND

EVERYONE KEEPS
TELLING ME
TO GROW UP—

but you,

YOU MAKE ME
BELIEVE
IN FAIRYTALES

r.clift

I HAVE TO ADMIT,
I'D ALWAYS HOPED THAT NO MATTER
HOW MUCH TIME HAD PASSED
OR HOW FAR APART WE DRIFTED—

it would be me and you
IN THE END

TO FEEL *anything* AT ALL

MAYBE NOTHING ENDS
AND FOREVER REALLY IS FOREVER—
WITH OR WITHOUT US

MAYBE THE END IS ONLY
ANOTHER BEGINNING—
A DARKENED DOOR
TO A NEW LIFE
DISGUISED AS PAINFUL DEATH—
ONLY TO TURN OUT
TO BE A SECOND BIRTH

MAYBE THAT MEANS WE
WILL NEVER REALLY END
BUT INSTEAD—
IN THIS LIFE AND THE NEXT
and the next and the next
WE WILL ALWAYS
FOREVER
BE BEGINNING

r.clift

IF I CANNOT SET YOU FREE
FROM THIS CAGE YOU'VE BUILT
AROUND YOUR HEART— THEN
allow me to set you free
FROM THE CONSTRAINTS OF
TIME ITSELF.

WITH THE STROKE
OF MY PEN I WILL INSCRIBE YOU
INTO INFINITY. MY LOVE,
I WILL MAKE YOU IMMORTAL.

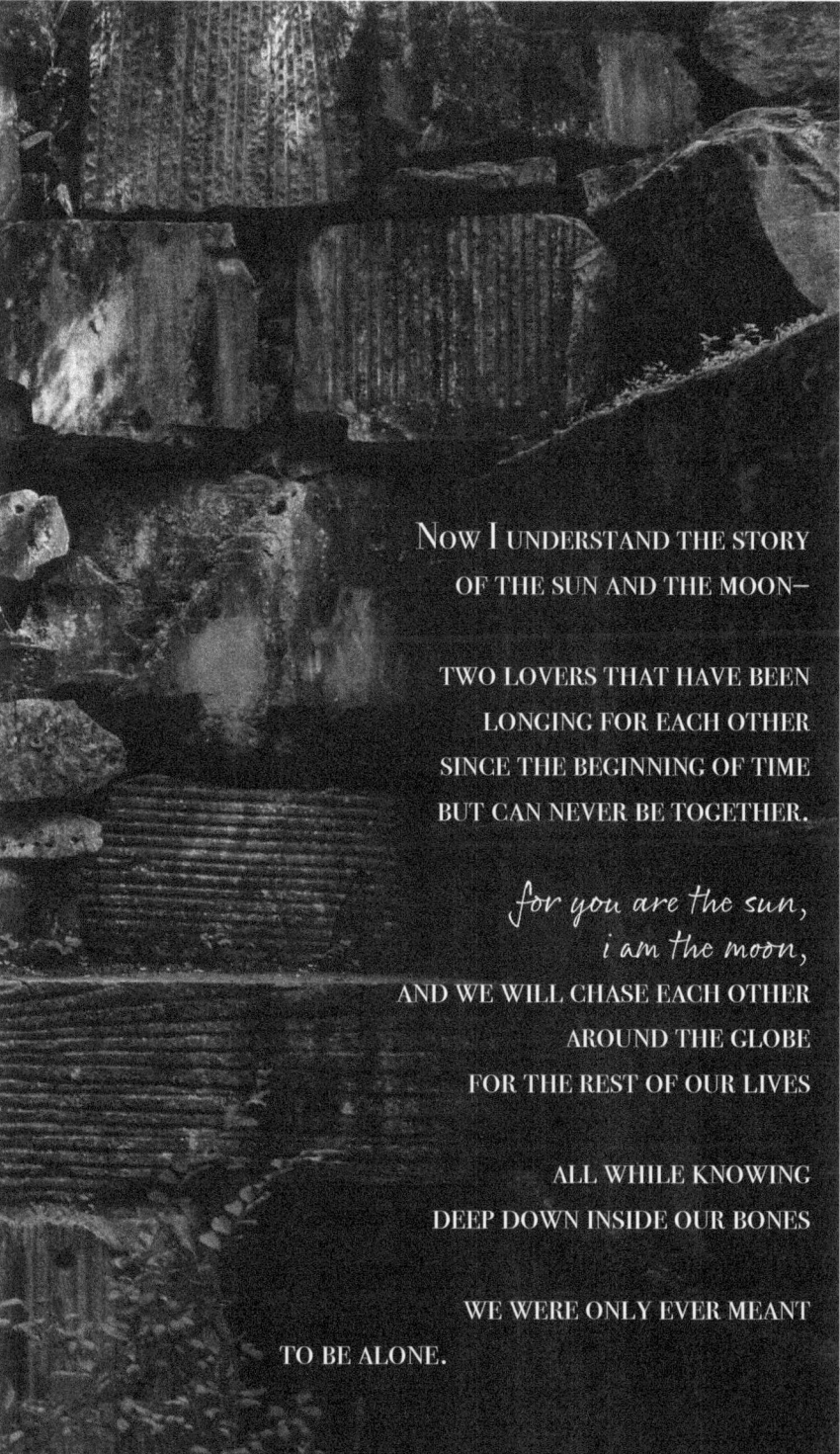

Now I understand the story
of the sun and the moon—

two lovers that have been
longing for each other
since the beginning of time
but can never be together.

*for you are the sun,
i am the moon,*
and we will chase each other
around the globe
for the rest of our lives

all while knowing
deep down inside our bones

we were only ever meant
to be alone.

r.clift

WE

MUST

BE

RESTLESS

UNTIL

THE

DAY

WE

TURN

TO

STONE

TO FEEL *anything* AT ALL

you

WERE NO ACCIDENT
NO COINCIDENCE OF THE COSMOS
OR HAPPENSTANCE OF FATE
YOU WERE PLANNED, CAREFULLY, METICULOUSLY,
AS IF THESE PATHS WE WALK
WERE LAID TO CROSS AT THIS POINT
IN THE UNIVERSE FROM THE VERY BEGINNING—

LIKE TWO PREDESTINED STARS COLLIDING
EVEN IF FOR ONLY A MOMENT

FOR THIS MOMENT WILL LAST
LONG AFTER WE'VE GONE
*(because just like you and i
some stars align only once)*

BUT NO MATTER THE TIME THAT PASSES
I WILL NOT SOON FORGET THE WAY IT FELT
WHEN I FIRST SAW YOU—

IT FELT LIKE COMING HOME.

r.clift

AS MONTHS BLEED INTO YEARS
I BEGIN TO WONDER
IF I WILL EVER FIND
another heart that beats
SO WELL NEXT TO MINE

TO FEEL *anything* AT ALL

WE ARE TETHERED, LIKE THE STARS IN THE NIGHT SKY WRAPPED IN STRING, CONNECTED THROUGH THE COSMOS— A KNOT AROUND OUR HEARTS PULLING TIGHTER WHENEVER WE TRY TO WALK AWAY FROM EACH OTHER. ALWAYS PULLING TIGHTER TO REMIND US THAT WE ARE BOUND BY THE UNIVERSE— NO MATTER WHERE WE GO, WHAT WE DO, WHO WE LOVE— WE. ARE. BOUND.

WE ARE INEVITABLE.

TO FEEL *anything* AT ALL

THE NEXT TIME YOU LOOK UP
AT THE NIGHT SKY
AND THINK HOW LUCKY YOU ARE
TO SEE A FALLING STAR,
REMEMBER—

THE STARS ARE GAZING
BACK DOWN ON YOU
THINKING HOW LUCKY THEY ARE
to see such a beautiful thing

SHINING RELENTLESSLY
THROUGH THE DARK.

TO FEEL *anything* AT ALL

*i am who i am
and if you
cannot accept me*
I AM NOT YOURS

r.clift

THE DIFFERENCE BETWEEN
ME AND YOU
IS I BELIEVE
temporary is worth it

LIKE PICKING WILDFLOWERS
OR FALLING FOR EACH OTHER

EVEN IF IT MEANS
A LITTLE PAIN

AND BEAUTIFUL THINGS DYING
IN THE END

TO FEEL *anything* AT ALL

YOU ONCE TOLD ME A STORY
OF WHEN YOU WERE YOUNG
AND HOW YOU CHASED A BUTTERFLY
AROUND YOUR MOTHER'S GARDEN
ALL AFTERNOON UNTIL
YOU FINALLY CAUGHT IT—

IT'S BEAUTY, FREEDOM, AND MYSTERY
was all there in your hands
BUT IN YOUR EXCITEMENT
YOU HELD ON TOO TIGHT,
REMEMBER?
AND WHEN YOU OPENED
YOUR FINGERS
HER WINGS WERE
CRUSHED—

THAT'S WHY I'M AFRAID
OF GIVING YOU MY HEART

r.clift

i don't stay for long

i delve into souls
give all i can
take what i need

and leave

DO YOU STILL
THINK OF HIM?

Silly girl.

HE WAS NEVER
GOING TO STAY.

SO WHAT?
YOU FELL IN LOVE WITH SOMEONE.
YOU MISS HIM? THEN MISS HIM.
TRY THIS, WRITE HIM A LETTER EVERY TIME YOU REMEMBER
YOU'RE STILL IN LOVE WITH HIM UNTIL YOU STOP CARRYING A PEN
WITH YOU EVERYWHERE YOU GO.

EVENTUALLY, YOU WON'T HAVE ANYMORE WORDS TO SAY.
one day you won't love him any more
AND AS YOU TOSS THE PILE OF UNSENT LETTERS INTO
THE RIVER, ONE BY ONE,
DON'T THINK OF IT AS LETTING GO—
THINK OF IT AS
SETTING YOURSELF FREE

MANY THINGS ARE TAKEN FOR GRANTED,
but love must not be one of them.
IT SHOULD ALWAYS FEEL
LIKE THE FIRST AND LAST TIME—
SO KISS ME. LIKE YOU MEAN IT.

r.clift

BE BOLD WITH YOUR HEART
AND TAKE RISKS DESPITE THE FEAR

life doesn't pass without pain

SO WE MIGHT AS WELL PRETEND
WE HAVE CONTROL

TO FEEL *anything* AT ALL

IN THE MORNING,
IF YOU FIRST WAKE UP
TOGETHER

AND THE MAGIC IS GONE—
then something is very wrong,
FOR THE MOMENT THE SUN
BRUSHES ACROSS HIS SKIN

SHOULD BE THE MOMENT
WHEN THE MAGIC BEGINS

r.clift

YOU PRESSED YOUR EAR DOWN TO MY CHEST
AS WE LAID IN PERFECT SILENCE

YOU KNEW MY HEART WAS STILL
A LITTLE SHATTERED, BUT
TOLD ME ANYWAY HOW
it was beating fast

I THOUGHT ABOUT WHO BROKE IT,
AND REALIZED HE NEVER ONCE
STOPPED TO LISTEN TO MY HEART
BEAT
HE WAS FAR TOO CONCERNED WITH
OTHER PARTS OF MY BODY

YOU KEPT LISTENING,
ENCHANTED BY THE UNSTEADY
RHYTHM

*he never cared
about my heart
like you do*

TO FEEL *anything* AT ALL

MAYBE IT'S TOO SELFISH OF ME
BUT I DON'T WANT ANYONE ELSE
TO EVER
HOLD YOUR HAND

EVEN THOUGH I KNOW
one day
SOMEONE WILL

AND THAT SOMEONE
WON'T BE ME

I'D LIKE TO THINK THE DARKNESS
INSIDE ME IS ONLY INK
AND WHEN I'M HURTING
IT BLEEDS OUT
INTO WORDS WORTHWHILE

TO FEEL *anything* AT ALL

HUMAN BEINGS ARE FUNDAMENTALLY
BUILT ON HOPE:

WE HOPE THAT OUR LIVES
WILL FALL INTO PLACE
AND THAT LOVE MIGHT COME AGAIN

WE HOPE OUR MOTHERS
WILL LIVE TO SEE US GET MARRIED
AND THAT IT WON'T RAIN AT THE WEDDING

WE HOPE THAT TOMORROW
WILL COME
AND THAT IT MIGHT OFFER ANOTHER CHANCE

WE HOPE EACH DAY
BECAUSE IN REALITY,
nothing is guaranteed,
AND SOMETIMES HOPING
FOR THE BEST
IS THE BEST WE CAN HOPE TO DO.

r.clift

IT'S BEEN CENTURIES— YET HERE WE ARE
STILL GAZING AT THE NIGHT SKY AS IF
FOR THE VERY FIRST TIME.

WE KNOW WE WILL NEVER FULLY COMPREHEND
WHAT WE SEE
BUT THAT DOESN'T MATTER.

I IMAGINE WHAT IT WOULD BE LIKE
IF WE COULD LOOK TO OUR FUTURES IN THE
SAME WAY
AS WE LAY BENEATH A SKY FULL OF STARS—
INSTEAD OF ENVISIONING FEAR AND DOUBT
*we would see hope
and endless possibilities.*

IT'S TRUE, YOU KNOW,
EVERY SINGLE DAY OF THE INEVITABLE
HAS THE POTENTIAL TO SHINE
AS BRIGHT AS THE SUN

IF ONLY YOU COULD SEE PAST THE DARKNESS.

I'M ON THE ROAD

TO HEALING

AND THERE IS NO

TURNING BACK

Dear you,

Yes you, whoever is reading these words.
I am writing to tell you
that this isn't supposed to be easy. Listen for a moment.
i know you're hurting.
i am too.
The sad truth is, everyone is in some kind of pain.
Isn't it beautiful though, to feel anything at all–
TO BE ALIVE.

That terrible, wonderful pain
is what fuels you to do more, to be more
in this time that we are given.
So don't think of pain as something like poison
to get out of your system as fast as possible.
Think of it as gasoline being poured into a fire.
Into the soul that flickers within you.

You may look at me and say
i do not see the flame. All i see is darkness.
But darling, let me assure you that you are the
light in the dark, and you simply cannot see it
because it comes from within.

I CAN SEE IT. WE ALL CAN.
So, my love, believe me when I say
your light will continue to shine
through the good and the bad.
it will guide you.

TRUST IN YOUR FIRE–
AND DO NOT BE AFRAID TO BURN.

– r.clift

ACKNOWLEDGEMENTS

I'm not sure where to begin, but I know if I were to mention every person who has gotten me to this point, it would be like trying to name every star in the sky.
Here are a few whose light has shined brightest in the effort to guide me in becoming this writer, this lover of words, I never knew I could be.

THANK YOU to my parents and my twin sister, Laura, for being my support system and giving meaning to the word *home*.
THANK YOU to my dearest friends, my sisters— Lauren, Sarah, Olivia, Carley, and Vanessa for showing me what real, true, unconditional love is.
THANK YOU, Ryan, for seeing the magic within us and helping me to believe that it has been there all along.
THANK YOU, Travis, for teaching me to be honest and true with our words, above all else.
THANK YOU, My Angel, for touching the stars with me from the top of a ferris wheel and showing me that our wings have always been meant for flying.
"It all comes back to love."
THANK YOU to my late professor, Arthur Smith, who redefined poetry for me and taught me that truly living is the most important thing one can do.
"The inspiration is the best part of the poem and you had nothing to do with it."

travel photo Locations

London, England	6
Edinburgh, Scotland	7
Tintagel, Cornwall - England	10
Max Patch Mountain, North Carolina	11-12
London, England	20
The Highlands, Scotland	21
Folly Island, South Carolina	25-26
Folly Island, South Carolina	32
The Highlands, Scotland	33
Paris, France	46
Newquay, Cornwall - England	47-48
Biltmore Estate, North Carolina	49-50
Max Patch Mountain, North Carolina	53
Cliffs of Moher, Ireland	64
Paris, France	65-66
Tintagel, Cornwall - England	67-68
London, England	73
Glencoe, Scotland	51-52
Newquay, Cornwall - England	81-82
Paris, France	84
Paris, France	90
Jupiter Island, Florida	91-92
Newquay, Cornwall - England	108
Country Clare, Ireland	109
Paris, France	114
Max Patch Mountain, North Carolina	115-116
Newquay, Cornwall - England	121
Knoxville, Tennessee	124
Cliffs of Moher, Ireland	131-132
Biltmore Estate, North Carolina	133-132
Howth, Ireland	139-140
Tintagel, Cornwall - England	145-146
The Highlands, Scotland	147
Okeechobee, Florida	150
Newquay, Cornwall - England	151-152
Notre-Dame, Paris - France	156

Paris, France	157
Notre-Dame, Paris - France	160
New York City, New York	165-166
Glencoe, Scotland	169-170
Max Patch Mountain, North Carolina	171-172
Cades Cove, Tennessee	173-174
Biltmore Estate, North Carolina	175
Tintagel, Cornwall - England	189-190
New York City, New York	191-192
Glencoe, Scotland	199-200
Saint Michael's Mount, England	201
London, England	212
Newquay, Cornwall - England	213-214
The Highlands, Scotland	217-218
Dublin, Ireland	221-222
New York City, New York	225-226
Glencoe, Scotland	231-232
Loch Ness, Scotland	241-242
Newquay, Cornwall - England	245-246

ABOUT THE *poet*

Rachel Clift is a writer and photographer based in the mountains of East Tennessee. She can often be found in a local coffee shop scribbling in one of her journals or typing up poems for strangers in front of her favorite book store. More than anything, she longs to inspire people– in some way, somehow, to love who they are and live life courageously.
Bursting at the seams with dreams of flying again, it's only a matter of time before she takes off to experience even more of the world.
She is a firm believer that traveling with only a backpack and little to no plans is the most marvelous thing one can do and no matter how many times a heart may break– it will always keep beating.

*Thank you, my darling, for reading —
for giving these timid words a home.
Now go, trust your heart, and*
   BE EXTRAORDINARY

♡ xx *Rachel*

FOLLOW THE EVER-CHANGING JOURNEY

@R.CLIFTPOETRY ON INSTAGRAM
RCLIFTPOETRY.COM

WORDS, PHOTOS, & DESIGN BY RACHEL CLIFT

TO FEEL ANYTHING AT ALL COPYRIGHT © 2019, 2021 BY RACHEL CLIFT.
ALL RIGHTS RESERVED.
NO PART OF THIS BOOK MAY BE REPRODUCED IN ANY FORM
WITHOUT WRITTEN PERMISSION FROM THE AUTHOR

FIRST EDITION, JUNE 21, 2019
SECOND EDITION, JUNE 21, 2021

ISBN: 978-1-736-96650-1

COVER ART BY LAURA CLIFT
AUTHOR PHOTO BY LAURA CLIFT

PHOTOS IN THIS BOOK WERE TAKEN BY RACHEL CLIFT IN
ENGLAND, IRELAND, SCOTLAND, FRANCE, THE EAST COAST OF THE USA
AND THE MOUNTAINS OF EAST TENNESSEE

Write your own poem here,
take a photo when you're done,
and send it to me.
{R.CLIFTPOETRY ON INSTAGRAM}
i would love to read your words.

xx Rachel

....

www.ingramcontent.com/pod-product-compliance
Lightning Source LLC
Chambersburg PA
CBHW040423100526
44589CB00022B/2805